Polar Animals

Written by DEBORAH HODGE
Illustrated by PAT STEPHENS

Kids Can Press

For Trish, a real Arctic adventurer! — D.H.
For Caitlin — P.S.

I would like to gratefully acknowledge the thorough review of the manuscript and art by Dr. Laura R. Prugh, Ecologist and Postdoctoral Researcher, Environmental Science, Policy, and Management, at the University of California, Berkeley. Dr. Prugh was formerly with the Biodiversity Centre, Zoology Department, University of British Columbia.

Special thanks to my editor, Stacey Roderick, for her important role in creating this lovely series. Thank you also to editors Lisa Tedesco and Sheila Barry for their ongoing support. To illustrator Pat Stephens and designers Céleste Gagnon and Katie Gray, many thanks for a beautiful book!

Kids Can Press gratefully acknowledges the financial support of the Government of Ontario, through Ontario Creates; the Ontario Arts Council; the Canada Council for the Arts; and the Government of Canada for our publishing activity.

Published in Canada and the U.S. by Kids Can Press Ltd.
25 Dockside Drive, Toronto, ON M5A 0B5

Kids Can Press is a Corus Entertainment Inc. company

www.kidscanpress.com

Edited by Stacey Roderick
Designed by Céleste Gagnon and Katie Gray

Printed and bound in Malaysia in 4/2019 by Tien Wah Press (Pte.) Ltd.

CM 08 0 9 8 7 6 5 4 3 2 1
CM PA 08 0 9 8 7 6

Library and Archives Canada Cataloguing in Publication
Hodge, Deborah
Polar animals / written by Deborah Hodge ;
illustrated by Pat Stephens.

(Who lives here?)
ISBN 978-1-55453-043-4 (bound)
ISBN 978-1-55453-044-1 (pbk.)

1. Animals—Polar regions—Juvenile literature. I. Stephens, Pat, 1950–
II. Title. III. Series: Hodge, Deborah. Who lives here?

QL112.H63 200   j591.75'86   C2007-902960-4

Contents

What Is a Polar Region?

A polar region is a very cold place. For most of the year, thick snow and ice cover the ground. Oceans freeze and fierce winds blow. The Arctic and Antarctic are polar regions.

The Arctic is home to many amazing creatures. Like all polar animals, their bodies are built for living in the cold.

Brr! Antarctica is the coldest place on Earth. Whales, seals and seabirds are the only large animals that can live here.

Some polar animals live on pack ice — large areas of sea ice floating in the ocean.

Arctic land is called tundra. Caribou and other animals gobble up plants that grow here in the short summer.

Emperor Penguin

The emperor penguin lives in chilly Antarctica. These penguins are taller than a kitchen table.

A mother and father emperor penguin take turns looking after their baby. The chick sits on its parents' feet, up off the icy ground.

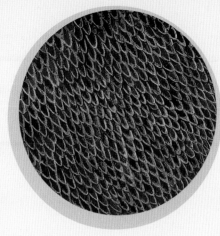

Waterproof feathers overlap tightly and cover the penguin like a thick winter coat.

Emperor penguins huddle for warmth. They take turns in the middle where it is warmest.

A penguin uses its wings to swim. It speeds through the ocean hunting for fish. Zoom!

Arctic Fox

The arctic fox is the size of a small dog. It roams over snow and ice hunting for lemmings and other prey.

An arctic fox's fur is the warmest of any animal. The white color blends in with the snow and helps the fox hide from snowy owls and other enemies.

The fox uses its tail to cover its face like a cozy scarf while it sleeps. Zzz ...

Thick fur grows on the top and bottom of the fox's paws to keep its feet warm.

Like all arctic foxes, this young pup's fur will change to white when winter comes.

Seal

The seal is an excellent swimmer. Seals have smooth bodies that glide easily through the polar oceans.

Some seals live under the ice for most of the year. In spring, a mother gives birth on the ice but quickly returns to the sea with her pup.

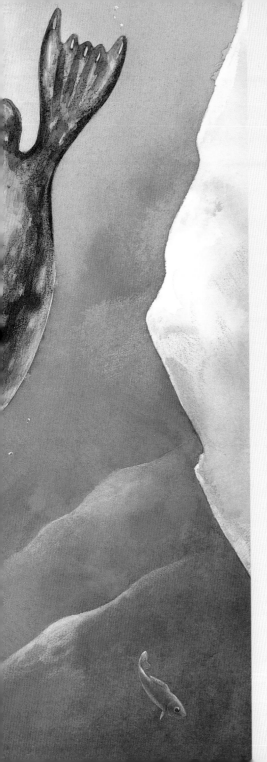

Swinging its back flippers from side to side, a seal races through the ocean hunting for fish.

A seal uses its sharp claws or teeth to cut a breathing hole in the ice. Now it can pop up and breathe.

Some pups are born inside a snow den. Shh ... It's a good place to hide from hungry polar bears.

Snowy Owl

The snowy owl is a fierce hunter. These owls perch on rocks and hills on the tundra to watch for their prey.

Whoosh! With its big wings outstretched, a snowy owl swoops down on lemmings, birds, hares and other small animals.

Snowy owls use sharp claws called talons to catch lemmings and other prey.

The owl's white feathers blend in with the snowy land and help it stay hidden.

Dark feathers match the colors of the tundra and help young owlets hide from enemies.

Musk Ox

The musk ox has long, shaggy fur to keep it warm. Musk oxen live on the tundra in big groups called herds.

Mmm ... A baby musk ox stays close to its mother to keep snug and warm until its own long fur grows in.

Soft, short fur under the long fur gives extra protection against the wind and cold.

Male musk oxen butt heads and horns to decide who is the biggest and strongest.

A musk ox uses its big front hoof like a shovel to dig up tasty plants buried under the snow.

Beluga Whale

The beluga whale swims in the icy Arctic Ocean. Belugas eat fish and other creatures that live in the water.

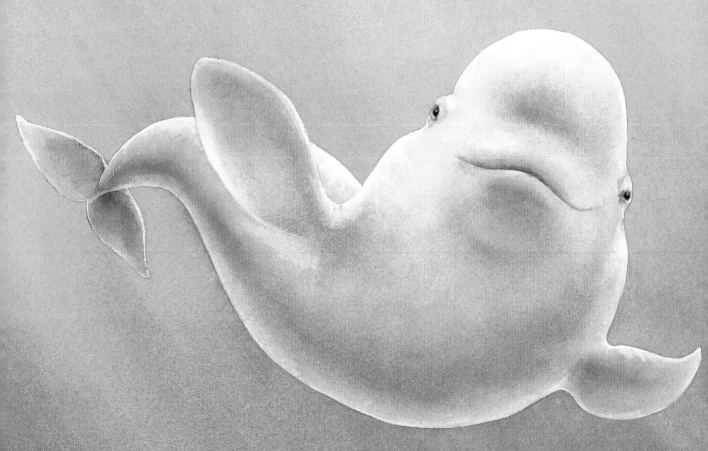

A beluga lives in a group called a pod. The whales in the pod talk to each other using sounds such as chirps, whistles and squeals.

A beluga breathes through a hole on the top of its head. Belugas poke their heads out of the water to get air.

Blubber, a thick layer of fat under the beluga's skin, works like a warm blanket to keep out the cold. Ahh ...

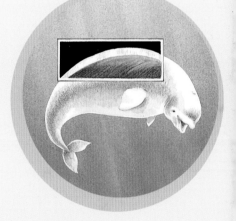

As a baby beluga gets older, its gray skin will turn white like its parents.

Polar Bear

The polar bear is a powerful hunter. Polar bears prowl over pack ice and swim in the ocean hunting for seals.

Polar bear cubs are born in a snow den. When they are old enough, their mother teaches them how to hunt and stay safe.

A hungry polar bear waits by a breathing hole. When a seal comes up for air, the bear pounces!

A layer of blubber under the polar bear's skin keeps it warm in ice cold water. Splish, splash!

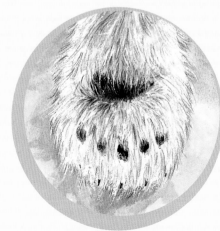

Polar bears can run very fast. Fur on the bottom of each paw keeps them from slipping.

Walrus

The walrus is a large animal with long teeth called tusks. Walruses live in the freezing polar water near pack ice.

Walruses spend most of their time in the chilly ocean but climb onto ice or rocky shores to rest and give birth.